# CONTENTS

# SEA MONSTER SAFARI

Are you ready to journey into a terrifying undersea world? You are about to set off on a safari to explore a mysterious part of the ocean. Reports suggest that prehistoric predators – thought to have died out millions of years ago – still swim here. Your mission is to photograph such horrors as giant sea scorpions, monstrous ancient sharks and ravenous reptiles.

You plan to use scuba gear to explore shallow waters. You will use a submersible to view deeper, more dangerous areas. You hope that the submersible is strong enough to withstand attacks from giant prehistoric sharks and meat-eating reptiles.

More than anything, you hope that you will see a creature nicknamed the 'Monster'. The deadly *Liopleurodon* is the *Tyrannosaurus rex* of the sea!

## SAFARI ESSENTIALS

**Scuba equipment** Your scuba-diving equipment includes a shark deterrent shield, which uses a small electric field to keep predators away.

**Camera** This hand-held underwater camera is for your scuba dives. The submersible also has a video camera fitted.

**dinoPad** Your special prehistoric e-book reader will be very useful — all known information on underwater prehistoric life has been uploaded.

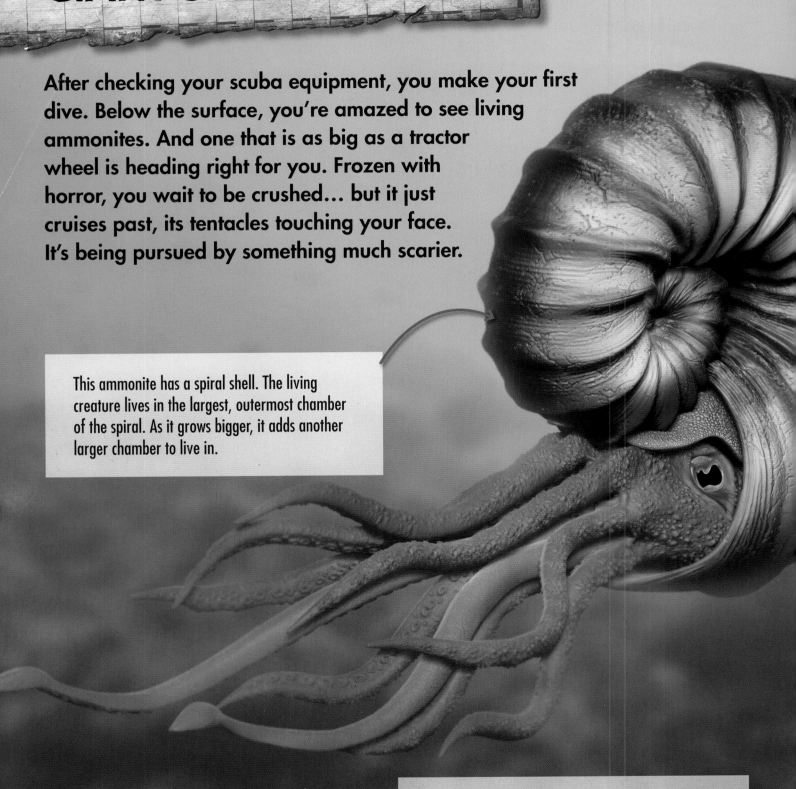

# GIANT SNAILS

After checking your scuba equipment, you make your first dive. Below the surface, you're amazed to see living ammonites. And one that is as big as a tractor wheel is heading right for you. Frozen with horror, you wait to be crushed… but it just cruises past, its tentacles touching your face. It's being pursued by something much scarier.

This ammonite has a spiral shell. The living creature lives in the largest, outermost chamber of the spiral. As it grows bigger, it adds another larger chamber to live in.

By shooting out water from a funnel-shaped opening, the ammonite propels itself through the sea.

Ammonite shells range from less than 1 cm (0.4 in) to 2 m (6.5 ft). The shells house slug-like creatures with tentacles; some 'slugs' are at least twice as long as you are tall.

# THE EVIDENCE

Fossils are the evidence we have that proves the existence of prehistoric wonders like the ammonites.

◄ **An ammonite fossil** forms after the mollusc dies and decays on the seabed. A hollow showing the shell's shape is left behind. Sometimes the hollow fills up with sediment that hardens into a fossil.

► **A cross-section of an ammonite shell** shows the chambers inside. By squirting the seawater out of some chambers, the ammonite can make itself more or less buoyant (floating higher or lower).

Ammonites are a group of molluscs. They are closely related to squids and octopuses.

**Meaning of name:** Named after Amun, an ancient Egyptian god who had rams' horns
**Size:** 1 cm (0.4 in) to 2 m (6.5 ft) diameter
**Family:** Cephalopoda
**Period:** Triassic to Cretaceous
**Found:** Commonly found in Cretaceous rocks all around the world
**Diet:** Plankton (tiny plants and animals)

◄ **The pearly nautilus** is the only known living relative of the prehistoric ammonite.

# TERRIFYING TURTLES

The ammonites are fleeing from two giant turtles – each the size of a car. These *Archelon* hungrily graze on jellyfish, then snap at ammonites that are too slow to escape. You bravely take photos. But soon, the only food left is you! You get the shark deterrent shield ready but fumble, and it slips from your hands. Then, out of the gloom, comes an unlikely rescuer.

*Archelon* is a marine turtle – the largest turtle ever to exist.

**Meaning of name:** Ruling turtle
**Size:** Around 4 m (13 ft) long
**Family:** Protostegidae
**Period:** Late Cretaceous
**Weight:** 2,200 kg (4,900 lb)
**Found in:** USA
**Diet:** Plankton, molluscs

The *Archelon*'s lightweight shell and strong flippers allow it to swim long distances into the open sea.

Like today's leatherback turtles, *Archelon* struggles up onto the beach to lay its eggs in the sand. It does this at night, in the hope that it won't be spotted by a hungry dinosaur.

# GIANTS OF THE TURTLE WORLD

◀ The giant *Archelon* is omnivorous. As well as eating jellyfish, molluscs and carrion, it also feeds on seaweed.

▶ The broad crushing surfaces of an *Archelon* beak can also crack open giant prehistoric mollusc shells, such as a 1.2 m- (4 ft-) wide prehistoric clam's.

▼ The first, 3.4 m- (11 ft-) long, *Archelon* specimen was found back in 1895. An even bigger one was found in 1970 at 4 m (13 ft) long! The *Archelon* holds the record as the largest turtle to have lived.

Its shell is leathery, rather than hard like a modern-day turtle's.

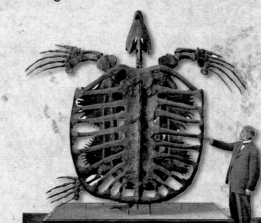

# DEADLY JAWS

The water froths as a sea reptile the size of a bus bursts into view, ramming the end of its snout right into an *Archelon*. The stunned turtle is soon trapped between its jaws. With a sideways thrust of the tail, the *Tylosaurus* carries off its meal. More *Tylosaurus* appear, snapping up ammonites. Horrified by this feeding frenzy, you swim away – it's time to seek the safety of your submersible.

The *Tylosaurus* has pointed, cone-shaped teeth for seizing, tearing and crushing. Two extra rows of teeth on the roof of its mouth help to keep a firm hold on its prey.

*Tylosaurus* is the largest of the mosasaurs, a group of fast-swimming prehistoric sea reptiles.

**Meaning of name:** Lump lizard
**Size:** 12 m (40 ft) long
**Family:** Mosasauridae
**Period:** Late Cretaceous
**Found in:** USA
**Diet:** Fish, ammonites, reptiles

Like other mosasaurs, the *Tylosaurus* has lizard-like scales.

Mosasaurs feed on ammonites, turtles, birds and even fast-moving giants, such as sharks and plesiosaurs.

# SWIMMING LIZARDS

◄ *Tylosaurus*'s name, which means 'lump lizard', refers to the rounded shape of the end of its nose. Combined with high-speed swimming, the nose makes an excellent battering ram.

▲ *Tylosaurus*'s powerful tail is flattened rather than rounded. This helps the creature to push its body fast through the water. A quick burst of speed is useful for a surprise attack.

► Mosasaurs have snake-like jaws that open extra wide so that they can swallow smaller prey whole.

# DEMON FISH

Between you and the submersible is a shoal of hideous fish. These huge, bony creatures, 5 metres (16 ft) in length, are chasing smaller fish at top speed. You swim on, hoping that they won't take a sudden interest in you – you could lose both your legs from a single *Xiphactinus* bite. You clamber into the submersible, sigh with relief, and lock the hatch firmly behind you.

A powerful tail gives this fast-moving predator a top speed of 60 km/h (37 mph).

*Xiphactinus* has camouflage colourings so that it can hide and ambush its prey.

*Xiphactinus* is often described as one of the most aggressive bony fish.

**Meaning of name:** Sword-ray
**Size:** 4.5–6 m (15–20 ft) long
**Family:** Ichthyodectidae
**Period:** Late Cretaceous
**Found in:** North America, Europe, Australia, Canada
**Diet:** Fish and other marine life

# DEADLY JAWS

► Unlike the jawless fish living alongside them, bony fish are able to bite into their prey and grip them in their mouths. *Xiphactinus* has a lethal, upturned jaw and fang-like teeth.

▲ *Dunkleosteus* has slicing bony plates instead of teeth, and an armour-plated body. It can easily attack and kill a prehistoric shark like *Stethacanthus*.

▲ *Coelacanth* was thought to have become extinct, like *Xiphactinus*, at the end of the Cretaceous period. But a living *Coelacanth* was discovered in South Africa in 1938!

*Xiphactinus* is both the predator and prey of sharks, depending on their size.

# LONG-NECKED SWIMMERS

Safely back in the submersible, you catch a glimpse of a long-necked creature, and set off in pursuit. You watch the *Plesiosaurus* swim, curving its body like a seal. The video camera records its sharp teeth snapping together around a fish like a trap. Now and then it lifts its head above the surface to breathe. After more photos, you take the submersible deeper, seeking the 'Monster'.

*Plesiosaurus* is a type of plesiosaur, which along with the ichthyosaurs, dominated the Jurassic seas.

**Meaning of name:** Almost a lizard
**Size:** 3.5 m (11 ft) long
**Family:** Plesiosauroidea
**Period:** Early Jurassic
**Found in:** England
**Diet:** Fish and other marine life

The first *Plesiosaurus* to be studied was described as a 'snake threaded through the body of a turtle' because of its long neck.

# THE LOCH NESS PLESIOSAUR?

► Some people believe that a large plesiosaur-like monster lives in the deep waters of Loch Ness, in Scotland. This photo, taken in 1934, turned out to be a hoax.

The long, sharp teeth interlock when the jaws close, to make a cage in which fish can be trapped.

▼ Another hoaxer claimed that footprints were found on the shore of the loch. These were actually made using a hippopotamus-foot umbrella stand.

▼ Many people say they've seen the Loch Ness monster. Some descriptions do sound like a plesiosaur: supposedly it has a long neck and small head, which leaves the water to take a breath.

The front paddles keep the creature stable. The back limbs push its body through the water.

# SHARKS ON PATROL

Suddenly, shadows darken your way. You slow the engines of the submersible as two sharks swim dangerously close. You photograph their greedy mouths. Using the dinoPad, you identify them as *Stethacanthus*. Their strange, anvil-shaped dorsal fins show they are males. One thumps its head against the glass. Terrified the glass will shatter, you dive deeper into the darkness.

*Stethacanthus* may migrate long distances, returning to waters where they mate and give birth each year.

Sharks are survivors. They have lived through at least five mass extinctions.

*Stethacanthus* is a smallish shark, noted for the male's anvil-shaped dorsal fin.

**Meaning of name:** Chest spike
**Size:** 70 cm to 2 m (2 ft 4 in to 6 ft) long
**Family:** Stethacanthidae
**Period:** Late Devonian–Cretaceous
**Found in:** Europe, North America
**Diet:** Fish and other marine life

# ANVIL HEADS

► Some scientists think that *Stethacanthus'* head bristles are meant to look like teeth in a giant hungry mouth, which might scare off attackers.

◄ Only males have been found with anvil-shaped dorsal fins. Perhaps they were used for showing off their power and strength during courtship with females.

▼ Fossil coprolites (prehistoric animal droppings) can tell us about ancient sharks' diets. We know that *Stethacanthus'* diet includes small fish and molluscs, such as ammonites.

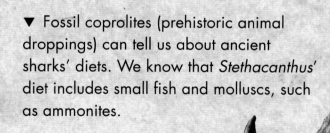

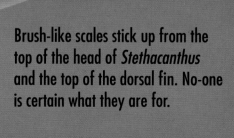

Brush-like scales stick up from the top of the head of *Stethacanthus* and the top of the dorsal fin. No-one is certain what they are for.

# FISH-LIZARDS

It's pitch black as you reach the ocean bed. You swivel the searchlight and there's a sight that makes you smile. You've seen so many ichthyosaur fossils – but this one is very much alive! It's the biggest ichthyosaur ever to exist, the 15 metre- (50 ft-) long *Shonisaurus*. While you're busy taking photos, you have no idea that something terrifying has swum up behind you...

The *Shonisaurus* is an early ichthyosaur, with a body shape similar to a whale. With this body shape, it could probably not swim very fast.

*Shonisaurus* may be huge, but it usually feeds on small creatures, such as squid-like belemnites.

**Shonisaurus** is an early ichthyosaur. Ichthyosaurs are aquatic reptiles that have a fish-like body shape.

**Meaning of name:** Lizard from the Shoshone Mountains
**Size:** 15 m (50 ft) long
**Family:** Shonisauridae
**Period:** Late Triassic
**Weight:** 40 tons
**Found in:** USA, Canada
**Diet:** Fish and other marine life

Ichthyosaurs have to swim to the surface to breathe — they do not have gills.

# AWESOME ICHTHYOSAURS

◄ The *Shonisaurus* has the biggest eye of any known vertebrate (any animal with a backbone). Each eye socket is 1 m (3 ft) in diameter. Each giant eyeball is protected by a bony ring.

▼ The first ichthyosaur fossil (a skull) was found by a Victorian girl when she was just 12 years old. Mary Anning was poor and gathered fossils for a living. Once, she was nearly killed by a landslide when fossil hunting.

▼ This fossil of an ichthyosaur flipper clearly shows its paddle-like shape.

# THE 'MONSTER'

The submersible shakes, and you grab the controls – you've been rammed! Your stomach lurches as the giant plesiosaur pushes you and your craft away. Moments later, its vicious teeth tear into the ichthyosaur's flesh. It's a *Liopleurodon*, the 'Monster' you've been searching for! You are delighted at last to capture your prize on film.

At twice the length of a killer whale (25 m, 82 ft), *Liopleurodon* is the largest flesh-eating vertebrate ever found.

Its cucumber-sized teeth (the same size as those of a *Tyrannosaurus rex*) have deep roots, giving it a very strong bite.

*Liopleurodon* is a large marine reptile and the biggest of the plesiosaurs.

**Meaning of name:** Smooth-sided teeth
**Size:** Possibly up to 25 m (80 ft) long
**Family:** Pliosauridae
**Period:** Mid Jurassic
**Found in:** Europe, Russia
**Diet:** Fish and other marine life

It uses its 3 m- (10 ft-) long paddles like wings to 'fly' through the water.

# TYRANT OF THE SEA

▼ *Liopleurodon* lives at the same time as *Tyrannosaurus rex*. However, the tyrant of the sea is almost double the length of *T. rex*.

▼ Using their limbs like oars, which they wave vertically, plesiosaurs virtually fly through the water. With extra effort from their back limbs, they can probably swim at about 10 km/h (6 mph).

◄ Plesiosaurs swallow stones to help grind down food and to act like the ballast in a ship. Stones in their lower abdomen give extra stability.

# DEADLY SCORPION

As you reach the coral reef, the submersible comes to a juddering halt. Something is caught in the motor! You swim out to fix the problem. An insect-like creature crawls stealthily towards you, flexing its pincer-like claws. It's a *Pterygotus*, a sea scorpion more than 2 metre (7 ft) long. Then suddenly, it swims off, flapping its paddle-like limbs in a panic. What has scared it so much?

*Pterygotus* has two pairs of eyes — a small, upward-facing pair on top of its head, and two large eyes near the front.

*Pterygotus* has two wider limbs to use as paddles for swimming. Its legs are not stout enough for much land walking.

*Pterygotus* can ambush its prey by lying hidden in the sand, with just its eyes peering out.

**Pterygotus** is the second largest sea scorpion (eurypterid) and a top predator in the Silurian and Devonian seas.

**Meaning of name:** Wing-animal or finned one
**Size:** 2.3 m (7 ft 7 in)
**Family:** Pterygotidae
**Period:** Late Silurian—early Devonian
**Found in:** All continents except Antarctica
**Diet:** Fish, trilobites, other marine animals

**Pterygotus** has strong jaws and an armour-like exoskeleton.

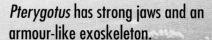

# MORE UNDERSEA HORRORS

▼ The giant squid-like *Orthocone* grows up to 11 m (36 ft) long and feeds on sea scorpions and fish. It can trap the biggest of sea scorpions with its tentacles, then pull it into its mouth.

▶ Trilobites scurry around the sea floor like woodlice. They swim upside down. Trilobites have a hard outer covering for protection, and some also have dangerous-looking spikes and spines.

▼ The biggest sea scorpion is the *Jaekelopterus rhenaniae*. At 2.5 m (8ft), it's the size of a crocodile, so you wouldn't want to get too close!

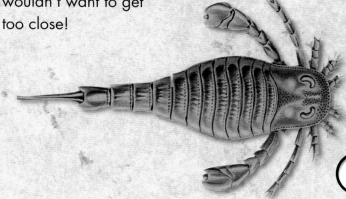

# TERROR SHARK

Two incredible creatures pass alongside the submersible. A vast prehistoric shark is pursuing a huge whale. You climb back into the craft, so that you can film the encounter. The shark grabs the flipper of the whale to disable it – and a violent struggle follows. You're suddenly thrown from your seat, as the 50-ton body of the shark hits your craft. A crack appears in the glass and water begins to trickle through.

*Megalodon's* jaws open wide enough for a person to stand upright between them.

*Megalodon* waits for whales to head to the surface to breathe, so that it can attack from below. The whale has nowhere to escape.

**Megalodon is the largest shark, is one of the largest fish and has one of the most powerful bites ever.**

**Meaning of name:** Big tooth
**Size:** 16 m (52 ft) long
**Family:** Lamnidae or Otodontidae
**Period:** Tertiary
**Weight:** Up to 50 tons
**Found in:** North and South America, Europe, Australia, New Zealand, Japan, Africa and India
**Diet:** Large ocean prey, including whales

*Megalodon* is two to three times bigger than today's great white shark. From 25 to 1.6 million years ago *Megalodon* was the top ocean predator – no other predator was powerful enough to attack it.

# SO MANY TEETH

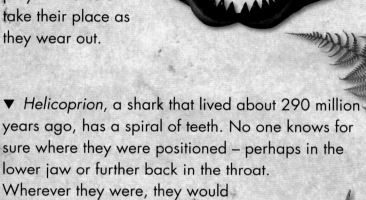

► *Megalodon* has more teeth than you may imagine – 276! They line the jaws in three to five rows. The front rows are used to catch prey. The others take their place as they wear out.

▼ *Helicoprion*, a shark that lived about 290 million years ago, has a spiral of teeth. No one knows for sure where they were positioned – perhaps in the lower jaw or further back in the throat. Wherever they were, they would make an efficient slicing machine.

▼ The biggest fossil teeth ever found come from a whale (*Livyatan melvillei*) that lived 12–13 million years ago. They are 36 cm (14 in) long!

# SNAKE NECK

The water inside the damaged submersible is already up to your waist, and you only just manage to pilot it to your anchored boat. As you set off home, you get to film your last safari surprise: these awesome shore-living reptiles, *Tanystropheus*. You watch amazed as one whips its neck around to snap up a fish.

*Tanystropheus* walks in shallow waters, then stretches its neck like a fishing line to catch fish or ammonites.

Its long neck isn't very flexible, but it is incredibly long — 3 m (10 ft) in all.

Tanystropheus is a shore-living sea reptile related to snakes, lizards and crocodiles.

**Meaning of name:** Long strap
**Size:** 6 m (20 ft) long
**Family:** Tanystropidae
**Period:** Middle to late Triassic
**Found in:** Europe, Middle East and China
**Diet:** Fish, other marine life, insects

Powerful rear leg muscles allow it to lean back and so stretch up its head.

# AMAZING ANATOMY

▶ Tanystropheus' tail can snap off if grabbed by a predator. This is a good way of escaping, and the tail will grow back.

▶ The teeth in the jaw of Tanystropheus vary according to its age: the young have teeth suitable for eating insects; the adults have interlocking teeth for eating fish.

▶ The neck is completely out of proportion with the rest of the body. As a counterweight (a weight for balance), there are extra muscles at the back of the body, behind the hips.

# SEA MONSTER SAFARI REPORT

On returning home, the world's top scientists are waiting to question you. You write a report and then agree to work with a television company to make a documentary. Your shots astonish the world – especially those close-ups of the killers of the deep, and their snapping, tearing teeth. Your own blood still runs cold when you recall *Liopleurodon* ramming your submersible!

The most awesome thing about the sea creatures you saw during your dives was their incredible size – shells the size of tractor wheels, turtles as big as cars, and sharks with teeth as long as your arm.

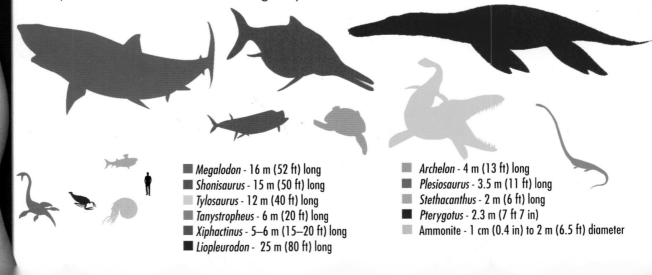

- Megalodon - 16 m (52 ft) long
- Shonisaurus - 15 m (50 ft) long
- Tylosaurus - 12 m (40 ft) long
- Tanystropheus - 6 m (20 ft) long
- Xiphactinus - 5–6 m (15–20 ft) long
- Liopleurodon - 25 m (80 ft) long
- Archelon - 4 m (13 ft) long
- Plesiosaurus - 3.5 m (11 ft) long
- Stethacanthus - 2 m (6 ft) long
- Pterygotus - 2.3 m (7 ft 7 in)
- Ammonite - 1 cm (0.4 in) to 2 m (6.5 ft) diameter

You plot the creatures you saw on a timeline and realise they lived at different times over a period of nearly 400 million years. In this chart, MYA stands for million years ago.

TODAY

| QUATERNARY | 1.5 mya |
| TERTIARY | 65 mya |
| CRETACEOUS | 150 mya |
| JURASSIC | 205 mya |
| TRIASSIC | 250 mya |
| PERMIAN | 290 mya |
| CARBONIFEROUS | 355 mya |
| DEVONIAN | 410 mya |
| SILURIAN | 440 mya |
| ORDOVICIAN | 510 mya |
| CAMBRIAN | 570 mya |
| PRECAMBRIAN | 4,600 mya |

Megalodon

Ammonites

Plesiosaurus

Archelon

Xiphactinus

Liopleurodon

Tanystropheus

Shonisaurus

Tylosaurus

Stethacanthus

Pterygotus

# GLOSSARY

**abdomen** The core part of an animal's body, from which the head and limbs extend.

**belemnites** Fossil shells that are several inches long, similar to the shell of a cuttlefish.

**camouflage** Colourings or markings that make something blend into its setting so that it cannot be seen so easily.

**carrion** The flesh from a creature that has died, which is eaten by other creatures.

**clam** A large shellfish with two main parts to its shell, similar to an oyster.

**coprolite** A fossilised piece of dung.

**coral reef** A ridge in shallow seas made up of masses of hardened material from the skeletons of tiny sea creatures.

**counterweight** A weight that acts as a balance, and stops an object or animal from falling over.

**courtship** A performance that some animals put on to show possible mates that they are strong and healthy.

**Cretaceous** A prehistoric period in which mammals and giant dinosaurs such as *Tyrannosaurus rex* lived on the land, and reptiles and ammonites lived in the sea.

**Devonian** A prehistoric period, also known as the Age of Fishes, when the oceans were warm and filled with many types of evolving fish.

**dorsal fin** An upright flipper rising up from the back of a fish, which is used for steering and stability.

**evolve** To develop gradually or naturally.

**extinct** Not existing anymore; for example, dinosaurs are extinct.

**flippers** Limbs used by creatures in the water for swimming.

**fossil** Prehistoric remains such as bones or traces (for example footprints) that have become preserved in rock.

**gills** The parts in a fish's body that are used for breathing.

**hibernating** Going to sleep for a long time just as an animal like a badger or bear goes to sleep during the winter.

**hoaxes** Tricks played on people.

**ichthyosaurs** Large sea-living reptiles that looked similar to dolphins.

**mollusc** A soft-bodied creature that usually has a shell in which it lives.

**mosasaurs** Giant meat-eating and sea-living reptiles that used four paddle-like limbs to swim.

**omnivorous** Able to eat both plants and meat.

**parasites** Plants or animals that live on or in another, from which they get their food.

**plesiosaurs** Reptiles that evolved to live in the sea and used paddle-like limbs to swim.

**predators** Animals that hunt other animals to kill and eat.

**prey** An animal that is hunted by other animals for food.

**reptiles** Animals that have scales and lay eggs, such as snakes and tortoises. Modern reptiles are cold-blooded; however, some prehistoric reptiles were warm-blooded.

**scales** Overlapping plates that form a protective outer layer on creatures such as fish and snakes.

**scuba-diving** An activity that involves swimming underwater using special equipment such as tanks of air to breathe.

**shoal** A large number of fish swimming together.

**submersible** A type of submarine used to explore the ocean.

**vertebrates** Creatures with backbones, such as birds, mammals and reptiles.

# FURTHER READING

*Dinosaur Encyclopedia* by Caroline Bingham (Dorling Kindersley, 2009)

*If Dinosaurs Were Alive Today* by Dougal Dixon (TickTock Media Ltd., 2007)

*The Mystery of the Death of the Dinosaurs (Can Science Solve?)* by Chris Oxlade (Heinemann Library, 2008)

*Naturetrails: Rocks and Fossils (Usborne Nature Trail)* by Struan Reid (Usborne Publishing, 2010)

*Sea Monsters: A Prehistoric Adventure* by Mose Richards (National Geographic Society, 2007)

*Sea Monsters (Wild Age)* by Steve Parker (QED Publishing, 2010)

# WEBSITES

*http://www.bbc.co.uk/sn/prehistoric_life/ dinosaurs/seamonsters/* Find facts and images of 21 sea monsters

*www.historyforkids.org/scienceforkids/ geology/eras/* Geological eras: discover when animals and plants lived through prehistory

*http://www.jurassiccoast.com* Kids' Zone – Watch a video: how do fossils form?

*http://ngm.nationalgeographic.com* National Geographic – search for the Bizarre Dinosaur section for a closer look at strange dinosaurs

*http://www.nationalgeographic.com/ seamonsters/* View sea monsters in 3D

# INDEX

First published in paperback in 2013

First published in 2012 by Franklin Watts
Copyright © 2012 Arcturus Publishing Limited

Franklin Watts
338 Euston Road
London NW1 3BH
Franklin Watts Australia
Level 17/207 Kent Street, Sydney NSW 2000

Produced by Arcturus Publishing Limited,
26/27 Bickels Yard, 151–153 Bermondsey Street, London SE1 3HA

Text: Liz Miles
Editor: Joe Harris
Picture researcher: Joe Harris
Design: Emma Randall
Cover design: Emma Randall

Picture credits:
Corbis: 2–3, 4–5 (composite with pixel-shack.com), 8–9, 29 row 3l. Dorling Kindersley: 1, 6–7, 16–17, 17tr, 17cr, 22–23, 26–27, 27cr, 29 row 6 r. pixel-shack.com: cover (main), 4–5 (composite with Corbis), 5tr, 10–11, 11tr, 18–19, 19tr, 20–21, 28t, 29 row 5 l, 29 row 5 r. Science Photo Library: 11cr, 11br, 12–13, 13tr, 13cr, 23tr, 24–25, 29 row 1, 29 row 6 l. Shutterstock: cover (top row), 5cr, 5br, 7tr, 7cr, 14–15, 15cr, 15br, 21tr, 29 row 2, 29 row 3r, 29 row 4 l, 29 row 5 c. Wikimedia: 7br, 13br, 15tr, 17br, 19cr, 19br, 21cr, 21br, 23cr, 23br, 25tr, 25cr, 25br, 29 row 4 r.

A CIP catalogue record for this book is available from the British Library.

Dewey Decimal Classification Number 567.9'12-dc23

ISBN 978 1 4451 2351 6

Printed in China

Franklin Watts is a division of Hachette Children's Books, an Hachette UK company.

www.hachette.co.uk

SL002124EN
Supplier 03, Date 0213, Print Run 2402

# PREH SEA MONSTERS FARI

**Liz Miles**

W
FRANKLIN WATTS
LONDON•SYDNEY